Stolen Flower

IRMA PINEDA

Stolen Flower

Guie' ni zinebe

La flor que se llevó

Translated from the Didxazá (Isthmus Zapotec) and Spanish by Wendy Call

A MARGELLOS
WORLD REPUBLIC OF LETTERS BOOK

Yale UNIVERSITY PRESS | NEW HAVEN & LONDON

Yale University Press books may be purchased in quantity for educational, business, or promotional use. For information, please email sales.press@yale.edu (U.S. office) or sales@yaleup.co.uk (U.K. office).

Set in Source Serif Pro type.
Printed and bound by CPI Group (UK) Ltd, Croydon, CR0 4YY

Library of Congress Control Number: 2025940602
ISBN 978-0-300-28248-1 (paperback)

A catalogue record for this book is available from the British Library.

Authorized Representative in the EU: Easy Access System Europe, Mustamäe tee 50, 10621 Tallinn, Estonia, gpsr.requests@easproject.com

10 9 8 7 6 5 4 3 2 1

Translator's Introduction

The story of this book begins with a crime: In February 2007, a group of Mexican soldiers raped a seventy-three-year-old Indigenous Nahua woman, Ernestina Ascencio Rosario, and left her for dead. She was working in her cornfield near her village of Soledad Atzompa, Veracruz, when she was assaulted. In spite of extensive evidence to the contrary, the Mexican government's investigation ruled that Sra. Ascencio died of natural causes. When journalists began to investigate the case, they learned that there were girls as young as twelve in Soledad Atzompa who were mothers. According to the girls' families, they had also been raped by soldiers stationed nearby. That is to say, members of the Mexican Army were terrorizing Mexican civilians.

Stolen Flower is a poet's response to systemic violence. News of that 2007 crime in Veracruz triggered a cascade of memories for the poet, Irma Pineda. She explained to me, "It reminded me of other situations during my life when the military was in conflict with our communities." In 1978, when Pineda was four years old, her father was forcibly disappeared by the Mexican military. Víctor "Yodo" Pineda was a teacher and leader in a regional Indigenous rights movement. Five years after her father's disappearance, the Mexican military attacked Pineda's hometown of Juchitán, Oaxaca, because the city's residents had elected the first opposition-party government in all of Mexico in more than half a century—a stunning accomplishment.

Pineda remembered, "In 1983, when I was nine years old, the army entered Juchitán to evict the popular government from City Hall, and a wave of violence broke out. I already had lived through my father's disappearance in 1978. In 1983, the presence of the army was much more public: they arrived with weapons; they established a barracks in Juchitán; they dragged women through the streets; they beat people; they imprisoned many people."

And then, eleven years after the military intrusion in Juchitán, Oaxaca, the Mexican Army moved into many parts of Chiapas, just southeast of Pineda's hometown. The Zapatista National Liberation Army marched into San Cristóbal de las Casas, Chiapas, on New Year's Day 1994, declaring war on the Mexican government and demanding Indigenous autonomy. The Mexican military responded brutally. "The army supposedly entered Chiapas to fight that armed group," Pineda told me, "but it actually attacked Indigenous communities. They went through the streets of villages and cities in Chiapas with their guns and tanks." Pineda visited Chiapas in 1994 as a representative of her Binnizá (Isthmus Zapotec) community; she witnessed the military presence firsthand.

In the following years, she tried to leave behind those experiences of violence. But Ernestina Ascencio's death in 2007 "detonated all those experiences in my memory," she explained. "I was filled with so much sadness and anger. All those earlier experiences with military presence in our communities were sleeping deep in my memory. In 2006 and 2007, when the so-called war against drug trafficking began, the army was again in the streets of our communities. In the end, the ones who suffer the most are those with the least ability to defend themselves: elders, children, and women." That detonation led to *Stolen Flower*.

Ernestina Ascencio's case sparked an outcry from women's and Indigenous rights organizations throughout Latin America. It catalyzed conversations about violence against women, about femicide, and about military impunity. *Guie' ni zinebe / La flor que se llevó*—the Didxazá-

Spanish original of *Stolen Flower*—has been an important part of those conversations. Critics throughout the Americas consider it a modern classic. The book consists of forty-five untitled poems, which some consider a single long poem: a denunciation of violence, a demand for justice, an appeal for reconciliation.

Irma Pineda published *Guie' ni zinebe / La flor que se llevó* in 2013. The book has circulated widely in Mexico and beyond. Prominent author and critic Ana Matías Rendón wrote in a 2016 review that the book "brutally reminds us of the essence of life. This book is a brave challenge to current times. If anyone knows how to deal with pain, it is Irma Pineda. She faces the world with the Word and shares with us her verses." The book's epigraph is an excerpt of a poem by Binnizá author Víctor Terán that directly addresses the soldiers responsible for the disappearance of Pineda's father, Víctor "Yodo" Pineda. Similarly, *Stolen Flower* addresses the soldiers responsible for Ernestina Ascencio Rosario's death and, more broadly, the soldiers who have perpetrated so much violence against Indigenous peoples in Mexico. In these fictionalized persona poems, the point of view shifts, including the women and girls in the community who were assaulted, other villagers, and the community as a collective voice.

Ten years after its first publication, *Guie' ni zinebe / La flor que se llevó* was republished in fall 2023 by Mexico's public education ministry, in an edition of twelve thousand copies distributed to public libraries all over Mexico. There is a bitter irony here: No one has been held accountable for Ernestina Ascencio's abuse and death; the legal case is closed. Mexico's federal justice system maintains that Sra. Ascencio died of natural causes, while another branch of government distributes nationwide a book of poems about her assault and the systemic violence of which it is a part.

In this trilingual book, my English translation of each poem is presented first, followed by Pineda's bilingual originals in Didxazá and Spanish. Pineda and I have collaborated since 2008 to bring her poetry into English. Pineda writes her poems in Didxazá and then, as she says, "creates new versions" of the poems in Spanish. She says of these two versions: "You must think of them as parallel poems, one poem created in our language and another poem in Spanish. Both versions uphold their respective literary traditions."

After sixteen years of collaboration, Pineda and I have a regular rhythm for bringing her poems into English. I create a draft in English, based on both the Spanish and Didxazá poems. I have intermediate reading ability in Didxazá and regularly consult with my Didxazá teacher, Friddamir Romero, about specific points of vocabulary, grammar, and syntax. I review my early draft with the poet, line by line. With each subsequent draft, I revise based on our discussions and then review it with her again. Pineda does not read or understand much English, so I re-translate many lines of my English versions back into Spanish for her, explaining my decisions. Because I can read both originals, I have two paths into English. Some lines of my English translations might seem a bit distant from the Spanish because I have chosen the Didxazá path. For example, the last line of the poem that begins "Night did not turn us to ash" ends with a reference to "the great tree of our wisdom." In Spanish, that last line reads "el gran árbol de nuestra memoria." The Didxazá word that Pineda expresses in Spanish as "nuestra memoria" is "xquendabiaanidu." That word is broader than what we would express in English as knowledge or wisdom. It also refers to something that is collective, not individual. There isn't a way to express that succinctly in English, so I chose "our wisdom" as the best among insufficient options.

Pineda recalls that as she was composing *Stolen Flower,* she read the news coverage and commentary about the murder case over and over. As I was working on this translation, I also compiled and studied all the media coverage I could find—nearly one hundred news articles from Mexico, the United States, United Kingdom, and elsewhere in Latin America—that have appeared in the years since Sra. Ascencio's death.

These articles report on the crime, the subsequent investigations of it, and the legal proceedings. "I cried a lot of tears with those news stories," Pineda told me. As I pored over the news coverage a decade later while translating these poems, I shed many tears as well.

Wendy Call
Colonia Centro, Oaxaca, Mexico
Mixtec / Zapotec territory
October 2024

For Cándida Santiago and Héctor Pineda.
For the blood, the pain, and the gift of love.

Ni icaa Na Cándida ne Héctor Yodo.
Lu tobisi rini, yuuba ne guendaranaxhii.

A Cándida Santiago y Héctor Pineda.
Por la sangre, el dolor y el amor.

For Víctor Yodo

Why did you take him
soldiers
that man who stands tall
his voice
him, the one we yearn for
my heart's north star.

Ni guicaa Víctor Yodo

Xiñee zinetu'
dxu'ca'
ba'du'guiichi zundí'
xtiidxa'
ni rinabala'dxi'
beleguí ladxidua.'

Para Víctor Yodo

Por qué se llevaron
soldados
al hombre, el de erguida espina
su palabra,
él, al que añora asaz
la estrella de mi alma.

Víctor Terán

Where is the precise place
that a man's heart might be split
before it cracks open
like an eggshell on the hearth?
          You repeat every night
in your green-stemmed voice
wounding the old willow tree's bark
          Who can return words to you
if thousands of footprints
lead away on the path
without even a moan in reply

Panda ndaa pe'
nga zanda guilaa ladxidó' ti nguiiu
ne qui xidxilaa
sicasi ñaca bichuga dxita neza lu bele ya?
       Rinaba diidxalu' guirá gueela'
ne ridxi cubi stiu' rului' ti na' yaga naga'
cayuniná ladi ti guesa yooxho'
       Tuunga gudxigueta' lii diidxa' ya'
pa ti xhiapa' duuba'
cabeeluca' lu neza
ne qui rudxiguetaca' ni ti ridxihuiini'

¿Cuál es la medida exacta
en la que puede dividirse el corazón de un hombre
antes de craquearse
como el cascarón de un huevo frente al fuego?
       Repites cada noche
con tu joven voz de rama verde
que hiere la corteza del viejo sauce
       Quién puede regresarte las palabras
si miles de huellas
asoman su rostro sobre el camino
sin devolvernos un solo gemido como respuesta

Shame floods the face of silence
        that just watches us
Some time ago our thundering voices
faded to small sparks
that sputter out each night
still reminding us
we were once bright blaze

Da' stuí lu guendarigani
                  cayuuyadxí si laanu
Ma xadxí nga ca stidxiguiibanu
gucaca' batee huiini'
ni rati guirá' gueela'
ti guedasilú laanu biuu dxi
gúcanu bele ro'

Inunda la vergüenza el rostro del silencio
                  que sólo nos observa
Hace ya tiempo que las voces de trueno
se volvieron pequeñas chispas
que agonizan cada noche
sólo para recordarnos que alguna vez
nos miramos fuego

Who are we now?
If the vibrant glow of threads we wore
has been masked by mud
to hide us from the poisonous
glare you sling
Who does your fiery breath hurt?
You might knock me down
       I might fall
but let me tell you
others will rise up and defy you

Tu laadu yana
Pa guendaruzaani' sti' ca doohuiini' ni gúcudu dxiqué
ma nazeca' beñe
ti qui gu'ya' guenda nanala'dxi' laadu
ne qui igaadu nisaxhini dxaba' ni rundaalu'
Tuunga' nalu' cayuninalu' ne bele riree ruaalu' ca?
Zandaca quiñentaalu' naa
       Ziaba'
xhisi gabeca' lii
ziuuru' binni guiasa gucaalú lii

¿Quiénes somos ahora?
Si el brillo de los hilos que nos vistieron de colores
hoy están cubiertos de fango
para ocultarnos de la mirada del odio
y del veneno que nos lanzas
¿A quién crees que dañas con tu aliento de fuego?
Podrás hacer que caiga mi cuerpo
       Yo caeré
pero una cosa te digo
otros más se levantarán para enfrentarte

Death's day has arrived
all light slipping through my fingers
I can't tell day from night
because lukewarm memory sweetens my soul
Could you carve the hour of my death on this tree?
When my spirit rises
it will return to this tree
to stare at your fingerprints
and pray you are forgiven
for the evil you planted among us

Ma bedandá dxi guendaguti
cuxhooñe' biaani' lade bicuininaya'
qui ganna' pa ridxi' pa huaxhini nga nuunu'
ti xidxaa guendaredasilú cusinaxhi xquenda'
Ñee zanda gucaalu' cue' yaga ca pora ndi' cayate la?
Dxi ganda guiasa xquenda'
zabigueta guriá yaga di'
ti guuya' xtuuba' bicuininalu'
ne guinaba' guiaaxha donda luguialu'
runi guirá guendanadxaba bindou' luguiadu

Este es el tiempo de la muerte
toda luz se me escurre entre los dedos
No puedo distinguir el día de la noche
porque la tibieza del recuerdo endulza mi alma
¿Puedes tallar en el tronco la hora en la que muero?
Cuando mi espíritu se levante
retornará a este árbol
para mirar las huellas de tus dedos
y pedir que te perdonen
por todo el mal que nos sembraste

Are you still a man?
Does any humanity survive in you?
Who are you now after donning
those steel-toed boots?
Your feet agile from marching for so long
But those stiff boots . . .
Ay! those boots that my body has known up close
now those boots command your steps
and carry you to the lip of the abyss

Nacarou' ti nguiiu la?
Nuuru' xiixa' nabani ndaani' ladilu' la?
Tu nacalu' yanna ra ma gucuá ñeelu'
ca guidibo'co' nachonga ca?
Ñeelu' nasisi ti ma stale guzalu' lu neza
Xisi ca guidibo'co' ziuula ca . . .
Aaah! ca guidibo'co' ni binibiá lade ra nexhe' layú
Ca guidibo'co' ca nga rini'ca' para chelu' yanna
ne ziné ca' lii ruaa bandaa

¿Aún eres un hombre?
¿Permanece algo de humanidad en ti?
¿Quién eres ahora después de calzar
esas rígidas botas con sus puntas de metal?
Tus pies son ligeros de tanto andar los caminos
Pero esas botas . . .
¡Aaah! las botas que mi cuerpo ha conocido desde el suelo
esas botas hoy dirigen tus pasos
y te llevan a la boca del abismo

I search your gaze to find yesterday's warmth
but your face is a hard clay mask
           I can't see your eyes
                 I tell you
and you don't care
because you only heed the voice
that has taught you to earn your daily bread

Cuyuube' ndaani' guié lulu' xidxaa gúpani neegue'
xhisi lulu' ca ma rului' cá beñe chonga lugiá'
       Qui ganda guyadxié guié lulu'
             rabe' lii
ni qui gannu'
ti ma runasió' xa ridxi
ni bisiidi' lii guyubu' gueta lu ca dxi di'

Hurgo en tu mirada para encontrar la ternura del ayer
pero tu rostro es una máscara de barro duro
       No puedo ver tus ojos
             te digo
y no te importa
porque no escuchas otra voz más que aquella
que te ha enseñado a ganar el pan de estos días

Bread soaked by tears turns bitter
You will eat it
and wash it down with booze
but you won't forget the taste of tears
        sluiced from the wings of fallen birds
that weep from the trees and settle on the flowers
like the dew that scatters the dawn

Gueta ni riu nisa ndaani' guendaruuna' raca nandá'
Ngá nga ni golo'
ne nisa dxu'ni' zaguibiruaalu'
ne qui zanda gusiaandu' xi naca guendaruuna'
     ni biaxha' lu xhiaa ca manihuiini' ni biaba
ni rietetí lu yaga ne ratadxí lu guie'
sicasi ñaca nisa rucheechena' telayú

El pan remojado en lágrimas se vuelve amargo
Comerás de él
y con aguardiente lavarás tu boca
mas no podrás olvidar el sabor del llanto
     arrancado de las alas de los pájaros caídos
el que escurre de los árboles y reposa sobre las flores
como el agua que esparce la madrugada

Stop following my footsteps
like a rabid animal
Stop sniffing the paths that lead to our home
like a dog on the hunt
We are not rabbits

                              not iguanas

                                             not deer

We are your mirror
See yourself in us and
know we are not your enemy

Ma cadi sa nandalu' naa
sicasi ñacalu' ti mani' duxhu'
Cadi guyubi xiilu' neza ni riné ra lidxidu
sicasi ñacalu' ti bi'cu' guuze'
Cadi lexu di' laadu
                 cadi gucachi'
                           cadi bidxiña

Laaca lii nga laadu
Biiyadxí chahui'
ti gannu' cadi laadu nga tindeneu'

Deja de seguir mis pasos
como un animal furioso
Deja de olfatear los caminos que llevan a nuestro hogar
como un perro de cacería
No somos conejos
                 iguanas
                       venados
Tu espejo somos
Mírate en nosotros
y sabrás que no somos tu enemigo

Mother   save yourself while you can
because memory this painful will kill
Leave with nothing
but the tender gaze of your men
buried under the devil's ear tree
Build an altar wherever you end up
to honor and bless your far-away dead
later you'll have time to retrace their steps
to remember them with howls
that would scare a coyote under a full moon
But go now
the men in green fatigues are coming for you

Bilá lii laga ganda   jñaa
ti guendaredasilú ni dunabé naná laaca ruti
Guyé zitu ne chiné siou'
xquendaruyadxí ca nguiiu' stiu'
ga'chica' xha'na' bezayaga
Ra guedandou' gula'qui' mexa' bido'
ti cu'ndaayalu' ca gue'tu' stiu' neca zitu nuulu'
ziuu dxi gutopalu' neza ni guzá ca'
ne gu'nalu' laaca' ne ti ridxi ro'
ni guchibi gueu' cayuuna neza lu beeu'
Yanna huaxa guyé
ti ca nguiiu' ni nacu lari naga' ca zeedaca luguiou'

Sálvate mientras puedas   madre
que la memoria cuando duele tanto nos mata
Márchate lejos sin llevar a cuestas
más que la mirada tierna de tus hombres
enterrados bajo el guanacaste
Al sitio que llegues instala un altar
para velar por tus muertos en la distancia
ya tendrás tiempo de recoger sus pasos
de recordarlos con aullidos
que asustarían al coyote frente a la luna llena
Pero ahora vete
que los hombres de verde vienen por ti

Your night-animal eyes don't scare me
as nighttime has also been mine
I have spread my roots through its body
          my ancestral guardians survive
          hidden in the underbrush
Your ferocious howls don't scare me
because eagle wings rocked my hammock
and a jaguar taught me his song

Qui ruchibilu' naa ne bezalú mani' gueela'
ca gueela' ca laaca stine' huayacaca'
ladica' huatiide' ca xcú stine'
        ca ni rusigapaca' ti xhiapa iza
        ca ni nabánica' xha'na' guixibeu
Qui ruchibi ca ridxi stiu' naa
ti xhiaa ti bisiá biniibi xquixhe'
ne ti beedxe' bisiidi naa riuunda'

No me asustan tus ojos de animal nocturno
la noche también ha sido mía
por su cuerpo he desplegado mis raíces
        guardianas de mil años
        las que permanecen vivas debajo de la hierba
No me asustan tus gritos de fiera
porque el ala del águila meció mi hamaca
y el jaguar me enseñó su canto

We are life
not history reborn
although you yearned
to erase
the color of my skin from the earth's hands
We are still here
in the dreams of flowers and birds
We are fire and sun
        warmth and light
lighting our path through wonder
        Warmth and light
that caresses our bodies during nights of love
        when man and woman become one
        to continue our lineage
making life anew

Guendanabani nácadu
cadi diidxa' ni bizacalú cabani sti bieque
neca lii gucala'dxilu'
nixiá
biaaniguie' guidilade' lu ná guidxilayú
Rarii nuudu
lu bacaanda sti' manihuiini' ne guie'
Nácanu guí ne gubidxa
          biaani' ne xidxaa
ni cuzaani' lu neza lade guendaridxagayaa
          Biaani' ne xidxaa
ni ruchaa ladi binni lu gueela guendaranaxhii
          ra gunaa ne nguiiu rácaca tóbisi
          ti guidale xpinnica'
ne chu'ru' guendanabani rari'

Somos la vida
no la historia que renace
aunque tu anhelaste
borrar
el color de mi piel en las manos del mundo
Estamos aquí presentes
en los sueños de pájaros y flores
Somos fuego y sol
          luz y tibieza
que alumbra los caminos en medio del asombro
          Luz y tibieza
que toca los cuerpos en las noches del amor
          cuando mujer y hombre nos hacemos uno
          para continuar la estirpe
y ser de nuevo la vida

Peace was our sister
until evil
eviscerated the earth
with its greed
Our cowering in the corner wasn't enough
our silent pain did not appease
A thousand crouching devils
dug up her body
to erase our history
and then claim
that we never existed on earth

Guendariuudxí nga binnilidxidu
dxi bedandá guendanadxaba'
biniibidxacha ndaani' guidxilayú
ti gucala'dxi' ñaparu' jmá
Qui ñuudxí di' necape' laadu dxido' si nuudu ti guriá
qui nidxá ladxidó' ne yuubadxí stidu
Stale binnidxaba' dopaca'
gundisa ladica' nannaa
ti nuxhiá ca' guendaredasilú
ne ti ganda gucaaca'
qui ñuu dxi nuzuhua'du lu guidxilayú

La paz fue siempre nuestra hermana
hasta que la maldad
sacudió el vientre de la tierra
porque deseaba más
No le bastó nuestra presencia silenciosa en un rincón
no estuvo satisfecho con nuestro callado dolor
Mil demonios agazapados
levantaron su pesado cuerpo
para borrar la memoria
y escribir después
que nosotros nunca existimos sobre la tierra

Silence shattered
when the devil climbed up from below
to touch the world's skin

He rose up in his green cloak
so no one could see his snake eyes
how evil dilated his pupils

The devil came in his leafy clothes
disguised as a child of the earth
wrung night's neck
          as she yelped like a branch snapped
and peace fled the grackles' nests

Guendarigani biruugu'
ra gudxi'ba' binnidxaba' ga'bia'
ti niga'na' guidiladi guidxilayú

Gudxibané lari naga'
ne guiruti yanda ñuuya bezalú beenda'
ne guendanadxaba' cusiaande lu

Beeda binnidxaba' ne xhaba naga'
nacu lari sicasi ñaca xiiñi guidxilayú
gudié yanni huaxhini
          ni bindaa ti ridxi guendariluuza na' yaga
ne bichiibi guendariuudxí ra lidxi bigose

El silencio fue cortado
cuando nueve palmas escaló el demonio
para tocar la piel del mundo

Subió con su verde manto
y nadie pudo ver sus ojos de serpiente
con la maldad dilatando sus pupilas

Vino el demonio con su ropa de hierba
disfrazado como un hijo de la tierra
apretó el cuello de la noche
          que lanzó un grito de ramas quebradas
y ahuyentó la paz en los nidos de los zanates

Fear nested in the children's eyes
        their closed lids blocking light
Smiles slip away
Cracking branches fracture sleep
Houses fall more silent than graves
The men arrive in the night
        wreck and scatter everything
Fear silences even the crickets
and owls don't keep watch nor hoot
We wish we were the wind
passing unseen

Bedandá dxiibi lu ca xcuidi
      iquelagacabe nanda cuchii biaani'
Ma zé xquendaruxidxicabe
Guendarilaa yagana' ruchiiña' bacaanda'
Ndaani' ca yoo ca jmá nayati que ra ba'
Laacabe redandácabe lu gueela'
      rusa'bicabe ne rindaacabe guirá'
Naro'ba' dxiibi rusigani berendxinga
ne ca dama' ca qui ruuyadxica' ne qui ruundaca'
Laadu nuudu gácadu sicasi bi
ni qui rihuinni ridi'di'

El miedo se instaló en los ojos de los niños
      los párpados cuelgan cubriendo la luz
Se han escapado las sonrisas
El crujir de ramas inquieta el sueño
Hay más silencio en las casas que en las tumbas
Ellos llegan por las noches
      todo tiran y todo rompen
Es tan grande el temor que los grillos callan
y los tecolotes no miran ni cantan
Nosotros queremos ser el aire
que pasa invisible

There are people whose hearts open
like ripe flowers that nourish birds
There are people with hearts of mud
mired on the path
        carrion tossed in the bushes
        dead fish forgotten far from sea

There are winged dreams that rise skyward
And dreams that fall to earth
and break open like squash spreading seeds
        shriveled by the sun before they can sprout

There are nights that escape
on feet light as air
There are nights that we remember
like words engraved on stone pillars
There are nights so long
                so very long
they could form rivers of tears

Nuu binni zuxale' ladxidó'
sicasi ñaca guie' ni ma biele' ra rigué' manihuiini'
Nuu binni ma guca beñe ladxidó'
biaana lu neza
       ruluí' maniyuudxu' bisa'bicabe gui'xhi'
       benda bisiaandacabe zitu ruaa nisadó'

Nuu bacaanda' ruluí' bisiá ripapa guiba'
Nuu bacaanda' riabantaa layú
ne rilaaca' sica guitu rucheeche xpiidxi'
       ni rucuidxi' gubidxa ne ma qui zandani

Nuu gueela' rié
ne ñee sisi bi
Nuu gueela' ni riaana dxiichi'
sica diidxa' gucuá lu guiebiaani'
Nuu gueela' ziuula
               ziuula pe'
zanda guchá ti guiigu' ne guendaruuna'

Existen seres con el corazón abierto
como flores maduras que alimentan aves
Hay seres con el corazón hecho fango
atrapado en el camino
   carroña tirada en el monte
   pescado olvidado lejos del mar

Existen sueños águilas que suben rumbo al cielo
Hay sueños que caen a la tierra
y se parten como calabazas que derraman sus semillas
   las que el sol secará antes de renacer

Existen noches que se van
con los pies ligeros del aire
Hay noches que se quedan grabadas
como palabras esculpidas en estelas de piedra
Hay noches que son largas
      tan largas
que pueden formar ríos de lágrimas

When the world pulled on its nightclothes
      the starry cloak
      we used to watch
      like fireflies hanging from the tamarind tree
they came
metal and flame in their arms
they set fire to the night
they woke up the earth with their savage cries
and the wounded-animal howls
      that flee
the noses and throats of my brothers

Dxi gucu' guidxilayú xhabagueela'
   lari cá beleguí lu
   ni ruyadxidu guirá' gueela'
   sicasi ñacaca' bacuzaguí nanda lu yaga tama
bedandácabe
ne lu nacabe nanda guiiba' ne bele
bicaaguicabe gueela'
bicuaanicabe guidxilayú ne xtidximanicabe
ne xquedaruuna mani' ni gucaná
   cuxhooñe'
neza xhii ne yanni ca bizana'

Cuando el mundo extendió su ropa nocturna
   su estrellado manto
   el que nosotros solíamos mirar
   como luciérnagas pendiendo del frondoso tamarindo
vinieron ellos
con sus brazos de metal y fuego
incendiaron la noche
despertaron a la tierra con sus gritos de fieras
y los gemidos de animal herido
   que escapaban
de la nariz y la garganta de mis hermanos

No wound hurts
like the silence
of those watching our flesh lanced open
      listening resigned to the crunch of bones
and show their concern
by mopping up spilled blood
so it won't dirty the dawn

Cadi cayuuba di ra gucana'ya'
casi riuuba guendarigani
sti' ca binni ni ruyadxí si cuxhalecabe guidiladidu
       riuudiagasica' caxidxi calaa dxita ladi
ne ti guluí' nuuca xizaa
rusiá ca' rinni xhii layú
ti qui naca' gacabiidi telayú

No duelen las heridas
como el silencio
de los que miran mientras nos abren la piel
       escuchan resignados el crujir de huesos
y para decir que les importa
limpian la sangre derramada
porque no quieren ensuciar el alba

You came with strangers to trample the grass
that only knows our feet
You blinded the sun
that had only gazed on my footprints
you slithered into the trees
to try and trick us
You think the world too weak
to escape your hate
you think the jungle too small to shelter us
because you steal her colors to paint your clothes
and use her leaves to hide from my brothers
   Ay invader
you don't care that
this forest is our home
it is our mother and daughter
we know every inch of her skin
just by smelling her scent
she doesn't want you inside her
and so
you will have no peace

Bedandalu' ne ca dxu' beeda guxhatañee guixi
ni runibiá' ñeesidu
Bitaagulu' lu gubidxa
ni huayuyadxí si xtuuba' ñee'
ne birendalu' ladi yaga sica ti beenda'
ti nalu' zacá zagui'tu ladu
Za'cuxou' qui zuganda guidxilayú di
ti guixaledu ra nuu guendananala'dxi stiu'
nalu' gasti gui'xhi' gusigapa guendanabani
ti lii gula'nalu xquendanaga' ne bitieelu' xhabalu'
ne riquiiñelu' xpandaga ti gucaachica' lii
          Ahhh dxu'
rului' qui gannu'
rari' nga lidxidu'
ndi' nga jñaadu ne xiiñidu
pa chu' xiidu xinaxi sti'
racabia'du guidubinaca ladi
ne laabe qui racala'dxibe lii ndaanibe
nga runi
qui susaanabe lii gasidxilu'

Llegaste con los extraños a pisar la hierba
que sólo conoce nuestros pies
Cubriste los ojos del sol
que sólo mis huellas ha mirado
y tu cuerpo de serpiente enredaste en los árboles
para tratar de engañarnos
Crees que no bastará la faz del mundo
para escapar de tu odio
piensas que no habrá selva capaz de guardar la vida
porque tú le has robado los colores para pintar tu traje
y usas sus hojas para esconderte de mis hermanos
       Aaah soldado
pretendes ignorar
que es nuestra casa
que es nuestra madre y nuestra hija
con sólo sentir su aroma
podemos reconocer cada parte de su piel
y ella no te quiere en sus entrañas
por eso
la paz de tu sueño ahuyentará

You will never sleep in the earth's embrace
Your conscience won't allow your eyelashes to meet
You are the unwanted
devil who sharpened his knives
on my brothers' necks
who stomped on my father's back
and broke night
into a thousand pieces now lost
and we no longer sleep in peace

Qui zasilu' ndaani' na' layú di'
Xquendabiaanilu' qui zaná iguiidi' guichalagalu'
Guiruti' racala'dxi' lii
binnidxaba' ni bituxhu gudxiu'
cue' yanni ca bizaana' nga lii
ni bixhatañee deche' bixhoze'
ne gundaa gueela'
ne bi'nini stale' ndaa ni qui guidxela yanna
ti ganda chu' bacaanda' lu

Nunca dormirás entre los brazos de esta tierra
La conciencia no permitirá que tus pestañas se junten
Eres el no deseado
El demonio que afiló sus cuchillos
en el cuello de mis hermanos
el que puso su pies sobre la espalda de mi padre
y rompió la noche
en mil pedazos que no encuentra ahora
para conciliar la paz del sueño

Wake up father
run with the foals already escaping
bravery is nothing compared to my desire to see you again
Can't you see the devil shadowing you?
Do you hear his steel-clad feet on the dead leaves?
Those aren't flowers in his hands
nor our ancestors' voices
Father he is thirsty
and wants to drink your blood

Bibani bixhoze'
bixhooñe ne ca mani' ni ma zé
gasti' nga guenda nadxibalú ti naa nuaa guuyarua' lii
qui ruuyu' cundaachi' binnidxaba' lii la?
cayunadia'gu' caxidxi ñeeguiibabe lu guixibandaga la?
Cadi gueta di nasa' nabe
cadi stiidxa' rigola nebe
Cayatibe nisa bixhoze'
ne rinni stiu' nga nuube guebe

Despierta padre
corre con los potros que ya escapan
que el valor no es nada frente a mis ganas de volver a verte
¿no ves que el demonio acecha?
¿oyes como suenan sus pies de hierro en la hojarasca?
No son tortillas las que sostiene en sus manos
tampoco trae la voz de los abuelos
Tiene sed padre
y quiere beber tu sangre

Don't hurry your steps mother
I too want to escape down the path
want to find other hearts
and speak without fear
But I can't leave so quickly
with the shadows of our dead
entangling my feet

Cadi nagueendape' salu' jñaa
naa laaca racaladxe' guxhooñe' neza sti la'dxi'
racaladxe' guidxela' xhupa' ladxidó'
ne qui chu' dxiibi ti guinié'
Xisi qui ganda saya' nagueenda
ti xpanda' ca gue'tu' ca
cucueezaca' ñee

No apresures tus pasos madre
yo también quiero correr a otros campos
quiero encontrar otros corazones
y hablar sin miedo
Mas no puedo caminar aprisa
con la sombra de los muertos
que detienen mis pies

Don't look back
even the trees are silent
Fear chokes them
as mute witnesses
to our spilled blood
They can't say anything to confront the evil
that imprisons their words
that smothers screams aching to soar

Cadi gutiixilulu'
ti ca yaga ca dxido' si nuuca'
Dxiibi nusigani laaca
cayuuyadxí si ca'
reeche la'dxi' layú
Gasti' zanda guini'cabe neza lu guendanadxaba'
ni nutaaguna' diidxa'
ni cayuutixhie' ridxi nuu guipapa

No mires hacia atrás
que hasta los árboles callan
Es el silencio que les impone el miedo
mudos testigos son
de las vísceras derramadas
Nada pueden decir frente al odio
que aprisiona la palabra
que ahoga los gritos que quieren ser pájaros

Watch out snake-dressed man
Watch out soldier
don't forget those unsnapped photos
of bodies scattered under the sun
like cattle lost along the trail
They are our family
those who will one day rise
from the dead
and return for you
demanding their mutilated arms
their slit throats
their broken ribs
their splattered brains
and the land drenched with their dreams

Biiya chaahui' ngui' naculu' lari beenda'
Biiya chaahui' dxu'
gupa ndaani' iquelu' ca banda' biaani' ni qui nibeelu'
sti' ca binni nexhe' lu gubidxa
sicasi ñacaca yuze biniti lu neza
Binnilidxidu laacabe
ne ziuu dxi ziasacabe
lade ca gue'tu' ca
ne zabiguetacabe ra nuulu'
ti guchacabe lulu' na' ni bigá
guebeyani ni gucaná
dxitacue' ni guche
yuubaique ni bixii
ne layú ni biuu gudxa ne xpacandacabe

Mira bien hombre disfrazado de serpiente
Mira bien soldado
guarda en tu memoria las fotografías que no tomaste
de los cuerpos tendidos al sol
como reses perdidas en los caminos
Son nuestros padres
los que un día se levantarán
de entre los muertos
y volverán a ti
para reclamarte los brazos mutilados
las gargantas laceradas
las costillas rotas
los sesos derramados
y la tierra regada con sus sueños

You stared at my sister's
belly like a plump fruit
And with a sure line
from north to south
you opened her to rip out her seed

Ndaani' benda'
biiyadxiu' sicasi ñacani ti cuananaxhi
Ngué runi neza guia' ne neza guete'
nandí pe' nalu' bichuugu lu' laa
ti gunda guxhalu' biidxi' nusigapa

El vientre de mi hermana
miraste como la fruta redonda
Entonces de norte a sur
con una línea certera
la abriste para arrancar su semilla

Who filled your heart with so much hate
that you are now blind to a smile
Who dried the honey from your eyes
so your hands would forget sweet touch
Who ripped open the earth beneath your feet
and let the demons out of hell
Tell me who did this
who made you forget
the love that can flow
in the rivers that lie
beneath your skin

Tu laa gula'qui' guendanadxaba' ndaanii' ladxido'lo'
yanna ma qui gannu' xiinga guendaruxidxi
Tu laa bicuidxi' nisadxiña gunda lulu'
ti nalu' bisiaanda' guendariga'na naxhi
Tu laa bixhale' layú xha ñeelu'
ne bidii biree binnidxaba'
Guni' tu napa donda
bisiaandalu'
guendaranaxhii ni ruxhooñe'
ndaani' guiigu' ni nuu
xhaguete guidiladilu'

Quién depositó tanto odio en tu corazón
que hoy no distingues la sonrisa
Quién secó la miel de tus ojos
para que tus manos olvidaran las caricias
Quién abrió la tierra bajo tus pies
para que del inframundo escaparan los demonios
Dime quién es el culpable
de que hayas olvidado
el amor que puede correr
por los ríos que hay
debajo de tu piel

I am the earth-woman you slashed to plant your seed
I wash my body to chase away fear
I wipe away red-petal fingerprints
from the sleeping mat's tender palm
I'm no longer the girl in bud
waiting for the day she would flower
in her lover's hands
You stole my flower
Soldier!
Plucked it without mercy
My branches lacked the strength to stop you
The rain from my eyes won't be enough
to dampen the soil
so my flower might again take root

Naa nga gunaa yu ni guchezalu' ne bisaananeu' xpiidxilu'
Yanna caguiibelade' ti che' dxiibi
Cusiaya' xtuuba' guie' xiñá'
ni biaana lu ziña yaa sti daa
Ma cadi dxapahuiini' mudu di naa
xa ni cabeza guendandá dxi ra na' xpa'du'
nga nuxhele laa
Zineu' guie' stine'
Dxu'!
Qui ñalu' naa bichuugulu' guie'
Ca yagana' qui ñanda nucueezaca' lii
Nisaguié ruuna lua' qui zugaanda
cu' gudxa layú
ne guni guiele' sti bieque guie' stine'

Soy la mujer tierra que rasgaste para depositar tu semilla
Lavo mi cuerpo para ahuyentar el miedo
Limpio las huellas de pétalos rojos
sobre la tierna palma del petate
No soy más la niña capullo
que esperaba el día en que las manos de su amado
la hicieran florecer
Te llevaste mi flor
¡Soldado!
Sin piedad la arrancaste
Mis ramas no tuvieron fuerzas para detenerte
La lluvia de mis ojos no será suficiente
para humedecer el suelo
y hacer que mi flor renazca

The animal of your hatred furrowed my skin
My eyes stayed silent before the old trees
I can't look in my sisters' eyes nor laugh with them
if my flower has withered

Mani' guendananala'dxi' bixhele' biní lu guidilade'
Bezaluá zagani neza lu ca yaga yooxho'
Ma qui zanda guyadxié lu ca benda' ne guxidxeniá laaca
ti guie' stine' ma naguundu nuu

El animal de tu odio hizo un arado sobre mi piel
Mis ojos guardaran silencio frente a los viejos árboles
No podré mirar el rostro de mis hermanas y reír con ellas
si mi flor marchita está

I stole lightning bugs from each May
to illuminate nights of love
you came and tore down the front door
       and smashed my jar of tiny luminaria
My sister tried to cradle them in her arms
but great fear wet the wings
of my bouquet of lightning bugs
and snuffed out their light

Guirá beeu' saa guidxi gulana bacuzaguí
ti ñuu biaani' lu gueela guendaranaxhii
ne lii beedandalu' binidé lu' ruaa yoo
       gundaalu' ra nucaache' ca biaanihuiini' que
Benda' gucala'dxi' nuguu na' laacame
xisi dunabepe' nuu dxiibi ngue runi ca bacuzaguí
bigadxeca' xhiaaca'
ne bisuica biaani'

A cada mayo le robé luciérnagas
para alumbrar la noche del amor
y tú llegaste volando puertas
       mi jarrón de pequeñas luminarias rompiste
Mi hermana intentó acunarlas en sus brazos
pero tanto era el miedo que mi ramillete de luciérnagas
humedeció sus alas
y apagó la luz

Earth woman I am
Earth opened
Earth slashed
Earth injured
Earth violated
Earth hurting for her sisters
Earth refusing to be plowed by evil
Earth refusing to cause pain
Earth refusing to give bitter fruit
Earth dying
Earth crying
Earth no longer wanting to bleed

Gunaa yu nga naa
Yu zuxale' ndaga
Yu ni guchezacabe laa
Yu ni gucaná
Yu ni riguiñentaacabe
Yu ni cayuuba laa ca gunaa
Yu ni qui na' guendanadxaba' guni dxiiña' laa
Yu ni qui na' gudxiiba' yuuba
Yu ni qui na' gudii cuananaxhi nandá
Yu ni nuu guibidxi
Yu ni nuu gu'na'
Yu ni ma qui na' guxii rini

Mujer tierra soy
Tierra abierta
Tierra rasgada
Tierra lastimada
Tierra violentada
Tierra que se duele por sus hermanas
Tierra que no quiere ser arada por el odio
Tierra que no quiere engendrar dolor
Tierra que no quiere dar frutos amargos
Tierra que se quiere secar
Tierra que quiere llorar
Tierra que ya no quiere sangrar

I am a woman
And I make sacred smoke
              Smoke that smells sweet
              Smoke that brings tears

Gunaa nga naca'
Laaca gu'xhu' bido' raca'
       Gu'xhu' ni rusindá' naxhi
       Gu'xhu' ni rusiguuna

Mujer soy
También incienso me hago
       Humo que aroma
       Humo que hace llorar

I am the furrow in the cornfield's skin
an open wound for planting new life
I am the blisters on the hands
of the men who plow at dawn
who open their eyes before the flowers do
who carry chipped water jugs
who wait for a smile
the sign of the cross made before them
I am the men of the earth's heart

Naa nga biní lu guidiladi ca ñaa ca
ni bixale' ti guiaba guendanabani ndaani'
Naa nga ti bitii lu na'
ca nguiiu ni richeza telayú
ca ni ruxhale' lu nirudo' guiale' dxi
ca ni riné xiga laa
ca ni ribeza guendaruxidxi
ni guzee luca'
Naa nga ca nguiiu binnihuala'dxi'

Soy el surco en la piel de los campos
herida abierta para depositar la vida
Soy las ámpulas en las manos
de los hombres que interrumpen el alba
los que abren los ojos antes de que se abra la flor del día
los que marchan con jícaras rotas
los que esperan la sonrisa
que dibuja signos sobre su rostro
Soy los hombres del corazón de la tierra

Night did not turn us to ash
       you set fire to the fields
       you burned our houses
but the flames did not reach
our great tree of wisdom

Cadi dé ni biaana ra biluxe gueela nga laadu
        gulaquiguilu' guixi
        bicaaguilu' ca yoo ca
xisi bele qui nungaanda
yaga ro' ni naca xquebiaanidu

No somos ceniza después de la noche
        incendiaste la hierba
        quemaste las casas
pero el fuego no alcanzó
al gran árbol de nuestra memoria

This is war
        you told us
and shot into the air
so all the birds would flee

This is war
        we told ourselves
and sharpened our words

Ndí nga guendaridinde
        rabilu' laadu
ne bicuaagulu' lu bi
ti guirá manuhiini' nipapa ne ñé

Ndí nga guendaridinde
        rabidu laaca laadu
ne xtiidxadu gulu'nadu

Esta es la guerra
        nos dijiste
y disparaste al aire
para que todos los pájaros se marcharan

Esta es la guerra
        nos dijimos
y empuñamos nuestra palabra

You declared war on us
  considered us scattered dust
  a feeble animal
  dawn's hesitant light
Now you know we are many
  friends of mountains and stones
  we know the rivers' language
  we speak with the seaside sand
Now you know we are not alone
  thousands of eyes watch from the jungle
  and see us dance with death
  and see you cry in the forest
  because you too know fear

Bicaa lulu' laadu
        nalu' yu dé reeche nga laadu
        mani' ma qui gapa stipa
        biaanihuiini' telayú
Yanna ma nannu' staledu
        xpinidu nga guié ne gui'xhi'
        runibia'du ni riní' ca guiigu'
        rininedu yuxi nexhe' guriá nisado'
Yanna ma nannu' cadi stubidu nuudu
        stale bezalú cundaachi' ndaani' gui'xhi'
        cayuuyaca' cuyaadu cue' guendaguti
        ne cayuuyaca' lii cayuunalu' lade ca yaga ca
        ti lii laaca runibia'lu' dxiibi

La guerra nos declaraste
        creíste que éramos polvo esparcido
        animal sin fuerzas
        pequeña luz del alba
Ahora sabes que somos muchos
        compañeros de las piedras y los montes
        conocemos el lenguaje de los ríos
        hablamos con la arena junto al mar
Ahora sabes que no estamos solos
        miles de ojos nos observan desde la selva
        y nos ven danzar junto a la muerte
        y te ven llorar entre los árboles
        porque tú también conoces el miedo

I won't need to wound your body
because even your tears won't bring
our dead back to life
nor will they erase
the pain of our memory
I can only cast my words
to the earth's four directions
so that sun and wind
can carve them on all the rocks
leaving no corner of the earth
where you might flee to escape
my voice like a litany
naming each flower you stole

Qui zunena'ya' dia' ladilu'
ti xquendaruunalu' qui zugaanda
gudxigueta' guendanabani xque'tudu
ne qui zugaanda guxhiá
yuuba lu xquendabiaanidu
Nisi chi gundaa stiidxa'
lu guidapa' na' guidxilayú
ti gubidxa ne bi
gucaaca' ni lu guira' guié
ne qui chu' guriá guidxi
ra ganda guxhooñelulu' ne qui gunadiagalu' stiidxe'
sica ti guendaruzee ruaa
cuzeete' guirá' guié ni zinelu'

No habré de lastimar tu cuerpo
porque tus lágrimas no bastarán
para devolver la vida a nuestros muertos
ni alcanzarán para borrar
el dolor de nuestra memoria
Sólo lanzaré mis palabras
por los cuatro brazos del universo
para que el sol y el viento
las graben en todas las piedras
y que no exista un rincón del mundo
a donde puedas huir sin escuchar mi voz
como una letanía
nombrando cada flor que te llevaste

My voice will weigh on you
like a rope hanging from your neck
My voice will be the vulture
that patrols your rotting body
and remains tattooed
among the sounds in your mind
so that you can't sleep
since you clawed the light
from our ancestors' eyes

Xtiidxe' zanaa luguialu'
sica ti doo nanda yanilu' nga zácani
Ti so'pe' canayubi
beela yuudxu' ni bi'nilu' ladilu'
nga nga zaca xtiidxe' ne ziaanani
die' chaahuini ladi ca ridxi ni rusigapa xquendabiaanilu'
ti guchibini xpacandalu'
sicape' lii guxhalu'
biaani' bezalu' ca rigola

Te pesará mi voz
una soga pendiente de tu cuello habrá de ser
Un zopilote que ronda
la carroña en la que has convertido tu cuerpo
será mi voz y quedará
tatuada entre los sonidos que guarda tu memoria
para espantar tu sueño
como tú arrancaste
la luz en los ojos de nuestros abuelos

Death's night won't come gently
we are shipwrecked in a sea of pain
no one should stay silent
because our cries will be the woodpecker
hammering your memory
                man in green
And when you try to close your eyes
you will hear my ancestors' voices
piercing your peace

Cadi dxido' di' zedandá gueela' guendaguti
laadu calaahuadu ndaani' nisado' yuuba di'
naquiiñe guiruti di' igani
ti ridxi ni biaxhadu zaca ti cha'ca'
ni quiide xquendabiaanilu'
                        nguiiu ni naculunaga'
Ne ora nalu' gutaagululu'
zunadiagalu' xtidxi ca bixhozegola'
caguiideca' guendariuudxí stiu'

No llegará en paz la noche de la muerte
náufragos somos en el mar del dolor
nadie debe callar
porque el grito arrancado será un pájaro carpintero
picoteando tu memoria
                        hombre de traje verde
Y cuando intentes cerrar los ojos
escucharás la voz de mis ancestros
perforando tu tranquilidad

Words and memory have more power than your weapons
We are the ancient tree that holds all history
in its every branch
Your green is a disguise telling lies
Perhaps you think we're nearsighted?
Even if we were blind
we will still hear the distant sound
of your body crawling
belly to earth like some worm
We know you will arrive like a snake
        spitting your venom
        vomiting fire
even after you incinerate our bodies
the rocks will burn with our memory's light

Diidxa' ne guendabiaani' jmá nadipaca' neza lu guiiba'
Nácanu yaga ni zuhuaa chahui' ne lu na' nugaanda
diidxa' ni bizacalú ca dxi ca
Naga' ni nelu' ca racala'dxi gusiguii laadu
Ñee nalu' nachepa' bezaludu la?
Neca qui nidu'yadu
zitu ca zunibia'du ra xidxi
caxuubi ladilu'
gui'di' layú sicasi ñaca ti bicuti'
Nannadu zedandalu' sica ti beenda'
           zundaalu' nisaxhinidxaba stiu'
           zadxi'balu' bele
ne gucaaguí siou' laadu
xquendabiaanidu ziaanadxiichi' lu ca guié

Palabra y memoria son más fuertes que tus armas
Somos árbol firme que en cada brazo sostiene
la historia de los días
Tu verdor es un traje que quiere mentir
¿Acaso crees que somos miopes?
Aunque fuésemos ciegos
aun en la distancia reconocemos el sonido
de tu cuerpo arrastrándose
con el vientre pegado a la tierra cual gusano
Sabemos que llegarás como serpiente
           lanzarás tu veneno
           vomitarás el fuego
y después de que calcines nuestros cuerpos
entre las piedras la memoria permanecerá

This dark night won't last forever
Nor will I listen to the silence of your pain
I don't want to hear your crying
Lift your eyes so morning will soon blossom
The sun will find us already on the path
Where will we go if our home is destroyed?
Keep going brother
The old trees replied

Qui ziaanadi' guelacahui
Ne qui zucaadiaga' guirasi dxi xquendarigani yuuba
qui racaladxe' guna' stiidxayuubalu'
Gundisalú ti ma yaca gueedandá' siadoguie'
Gubidxa guinaaze' laanu ma zuhua'nu lu neza
Paraa ndi' chuunu pa ma binidé cabe lidxinu la?
Guzaru' bizana'
Yaga yooxho' gucabi laanu

No será eterna la noche oscura
Ni escucharé por siempre el silencio de tu dolor
no quiero oír más tus lamentos
Levanta los ojos que pronto llegará la flor de la mañana
El sol debe encontrarnos de pie sobre el camino
¿Hacia dónde iremos si nuestro hogar fue destrozado?
Avanza hermano
Los árboles viejos nos responderán

Gather up your sorrows, my sister
hide them among basil's healing leaves
find the riverbank wending through our village
when you arrive at the dry bushes
turn your back on the water snaking its way
and toss all the branches over your shoulder
don't look back
the basil and riverwater
will carry away your pain

Gundisa' nabana' stiu' benda'
bisigapa laaca' lade bandaga guie' stia'
biyubi ruaa guiigu' ni ridi'dilaaga' xquidxinu
ra guedandou' cue' bidxummi
bidxii de'chu' nisa ni rizá sica ti beenda' ca
ne bindaa guie' ca lu xhi'quelu'
quepe gudxiguetalulu'
guie'stiá ne nisa
nitiicasi yuuba' zineca'

Levanta tus tristezas hermana
guárdalas entre las hojas de la albahaca
busca la ribera del río que atraviesa nuestro pueblo
cuando llegues junto al chamizo
dale la espalda al agua que serpentea
y sobre tus hombros lanza todas las ramas
no vuelvas a mirar hacia atrás
la albahaca y el agua
tus penas se llevarán

Let me hear your voice
        I'm not expecting sweet words
        nor asking for a prayer
I just want to talk with you
and tell you the histories we wove
among the legs of the forest's trees
Take off your mask
        let your weapons rest
I know you once sparked joy
in your people's eyes
I know you once chased butterflies
and tried to learn what
        hummingbird wings are made of
Where did you bury your dreams?
Give me your hands and calm your heart

Bidii naa gunebia'ya' xtiidxilu'
      cadi diidxa' naxhi di cabeza'
      cadi ti ndaaya' di' canaba' lii
Racaladxe' sia' guinie'nia' lii
ne güenia' lii ca diidxa' ni gudibadu
lade ñee yaga
Gulee ni cá lulu' ca
      bidii guisiila'dxi' ca xquiibalu'
Nannapia' biuu dxi gucalu' nayache'
neza lu xpinnilu'
Nannapia' dxiqué rizanandalu' biguiidi'
ne biyubu' gannu'
      xi bia'ne xhiaa biulú
Paraa nga bicaachilu' guirá ni gucala'dxilu' dxiqué?
Dané nalu' naa ne bisaana gatadxí ladxido'lo'

Conocer tu voz permíteme
      no son palabras dulces las que espero
      ni te pido una oración
Sólo quiero platicar contigo
y contarte las historias que tejimos
entre las piernas de los árboles
Quítate la máscara
      deja reposar tus armas
Bien sé que un día fuiste alegría
para los ojos de tu gente
Bien sé que hubo un tiempo en que tú perseguías mariposas
y tratabas de descubrir
      de qué están hechas las alas del colibrí
¿Dónde enterraste tus deseos?
Dame tus manos y deja que descanse tu corazón

Don't ask me to forget father
        while my wounds still weep
You can see the stitches on my body
        where I tried to sew my skin closed
I can't pretend that I haven't seen
        the uprooted and trampled flowers
My eyes still pulse with the bewilderment
        I saw in the children's gaze
My ears still ring with
        the cries from my sisters' mouths
Father don't ask me to forgive
        because scars always remember

Cadi gabilu' naa gusiaanda' bixhoze'
      ti ca'ru' guiiegu' ra gucana'ya'
Lade' zanda gu'yalu' ca doohuiini'
      ni racaladxe' gutaguania' guidi ni zuxale'
Qui zanda gune' naa sica qui ñuuya'
      guirá' guie' ni gúxhacabe ne bituñeecabe
Ndaani' bezalua' capaparu' guendaridxagayaa
      ne ridxela' lu ca xcuidica
Qui ganda igani ra diaga'
      guirá' ca ay! ni biree ruaa ca bizana'
Cadi guinabalu' naa gaxha' donda luguiacabe
      ti ca biaxhibeela ca nga cani'ca'

No me pidas el olvido padre
      que mis heridas aun no cierran
Sobre mi cuerpo puedes mirar los hilos
      con que intento juntar la piel abierta
No puedo fingir que no he mirado
      las flores arrancadas y pisoteadas
En mis ojos aun late el desconcierto
      que encuentro en la mirada de los niños
No dejan de sonar en mis oídos
      los ayes salidos de la boca de mis hermanas
No me pidas que perdone padre
      pues las cicatrices son memoria

No need to break a man's heart
to hear its crunch   my child
No need to place it before the fire
to see the cracks appear
and note its moment of splitting
Hate is enough to break it
      it's not the time that's passed
      nor the dead girls
      not the accumulated pain
      nor the people we've lost that kill us
Just that small moment is enough
for sleeping rage to stretch its arms
yawn
let out a tiny moan
and we notice a heart splitting
like an eggshell by the fire

Cadi naquiiñe guindaalu' ladxido' ti nguiiu
ti gucaadiagalu' xquendarilaa   xiiñe'
Cadi naquiiñe guzaabilu' laa neza lu bele
ti gu'yalu' xi naca lu ra chi guilaa
ne gannu' piou' ra xidxilaa
Guendanadxaba' si naquiiñe
          cadi ca dxi ni biapa' ca
          cadi guirá ni guti' ra deru' ziyale
          cadi yuuba' ni nutagunanu
          ne cadi guendaribana' nga ni ruuti laanu
Naquiiñe si ti ndaahuiini' dxi
ra gusigaa na' guendananala'dxi' ni nisiaasi'
ra guxhale' ruaa
cuee ti ridxihuiini'
racá nga zannanu' ti ladxido' nga calaa
sicasi ñaca ti bichuga dxita neza lu bele

No es necesario dividir el corazón de un hombre
para escuchar su crujido   hijo mío
No necesitas colocarlo frente a la fogata
para ver como aparecen fisuras en su rostro
y darte cuenta del momento preciso en que hace crac
Basta el odio para romperlo
          no es el tiempo guardado
          ni las jóvenes muertes
          no es el dolor acumulado
          ni las ausencias las que nos matan
Sólo basta ese pequeño instante
en que el rencor adormecido estira los brazos
bosteza
emite un pequeño gemido
y nos damos cuenta de que es el corazón que se craquela
como el cascarón de un huevo frente al fuego

Father I spoke to him
               to that man in green
I wanted to tell him we are equals
children born of red earth
I looked in his eyes to find
some trace of his ancient name
but he hid his shame
behind the colors he stole
from the forest's hands
I wanted to tell him our people's stories
to stir his memory
and push the huge stone of his body
but that man
               refused to reply

Naa gunie' nia' laabe bixhoze'
                    nguiiu nacu lari naga'
gucaladxe' ñabe laabe nguecasi laadu
ba'du' ni guxana layú xiñaa di'
Biiya bezalube ne racá biyube'
ti xtuubahuiini' lá ni gupabe dxiqué
xisi laabe cucaachibe stuí
deche' ca guendaridiee ni gula'nabe
lu na' gui'xhi'
Gucaladxe' ñuenia' laabe ca diidxa' xquidxinu'
tu nudxiee xquendabiaanibe
ne nuniibe' guié ngola nuu ládibe
xisi nguiiu ca
                    qui niná nucabi naa

Yo le hablé padre
                    al hombre del traje verde
quise decirle que somos iguales
hijos paridos por la roja tierra
Miré sus ojos para buscar
algún rastro de su antiguo nombre
pero él esconde su vergüenza
detrás de los colores arrebatados
de las manos del monte
Quise contarle las leyendas de este pueblo
para revolver su memoria
y mover la enorme piedra que ocupa su cuerpo
pero el hombre
                    no me quiso responder

If the man had opened his mouth's closed bud
if the flower of his lips had blossomed
asked to speak
coaxed words buried in the cavern of my throat
I would tell him:

        a person's heart can be divided
        countless times
        to share its love

And I would tell him:

        though he is the hand of evil
        he too

                is my brother

Pa nguiiu ca nuxhale' mudu sti'
pa guie' guidiruaabe ñele'
ti ninababe diidxa'
ti nibeebe diidxa' ga'chi' ndaani' bá yanne'
ñabe' laabe:

        ladxido' ti binni
        zanda guilaa bia'ticasi
        pa chi tiizi guendaranaxhii

Ne ñabe laabe:

        neca nacabe na' guendanadxaba'
        laaca
                bizana' nga laabe

Si el hombre hubiese abierto su capullo
si la flor de sus labios se hubiese extendido
para pedir la palabra
para llamar a la palabra escondida en mi garganta
yo le diría:

        que el corazón de una persona
        puede dividirse infinidad de veces
        para repartir su amor

Y le diría:

        que a pesar de ser la mano del odio
        él también
                es mi hermano

Translator's Notes

Pineda writes in Didxazá, the Juchitán variant of Isthmus Zapotec, which is spoken by perhaps one hundred thousand people in the southern state of Oaxaca, Mexico. The Zapotec language family has approximately a half-million speakers throughout southern Mexico and in Mexico City, in the diaspora in the United States—especially in Los Angeles and New York—and elsewhere in the world. Zapotec has a written history that stretches back more than two millennia. The Zapotecs were probably the first (and perhaps the only) society in the Americas to invent, rather than adopt, the technology of writing. They developed a glyph-based writing system well over two thousand years ago, long before their neighbors to the southeast, the Maya. Zapotec poets and writers have used a transliterated Latinate alphabet since the late 1800s.

The book's epigraph is from a poem by another renowned poet from the city of Juchitán, Oaxaca: Víctor Terán. He was an important activist in the social movement that Víctor "Yodo" Pineda led before his disappearance. Irma Pineda and Víctor Terán are two of a small number of writers working in Mexican (Indigenous) languages whose work is available in English. Víctor Terán's is in English translation by the poet Shook; the epigraph is my translation.

In the poem—or poem section—that begins "Mother save yourself while you can" (page 18), the English translation uses one of the lesser-known names of the guanacaste tree, *Enterolobium cyclocarpum*, also known as an "elephant-ear tree" for the shape of its fruit. A beautiful, highly prized tropical tree, the guanacaste is the national tree of Costa Rica.

The Didxazá word dxu' appears several times in the manuscript. It is most often used to mean "soldier," but also means "foreigner" in a pejorative sense or "invader." I have translated dxu' as either "solider" or "invader" or "stranger," depending on the poet's preference in each case.

The poem that begins with the line "Words and memory have more power than your weapons" (page 80) ends with a reference to the rocks that will "burn with our memory's light." This image is bicultural, operating differently in the poem's Didxazá and Spanish versions. In Zapotec cosmology, rocks are animate and hold collective memory and cultural history. Meanwhile, Latin Americans often say, "Carve it on a stela," referencing ancient stone stelae and also the permanence of rock over the ephemerality of paper.

Translator's Acknowledgments

I am deeply grateful to Adam Coon, Jess Fenn, Nadia Ghent, Friddamir Romero, Sejal Shah, and especially Adela Ramos for their extremely helpful feedback on parts of this manuscript. I also offer heartfelt thanks to three anonymous reviewers who wrote beautiful and generous responses to it, and to Abbie Storch and the entire team at Yale for their care. The thoughtful observations of my undergraduate students at both Pacific Lutheran University (on a study-away program in Oaxaca) and at the Pontífica Universidad Javeriana (in Bogotá, Colombia) about the original Didxazá-Spanish edition of the book helped me as well. My English translation of *Stolen Flower* was completed thanks to a 2017–2018 Wang Center research grant from Pacific Lutheran University, a 2021 Global South Translation Grant from the Institute for Comparative Modernities at Cornell University, and support from the MFA in Literary Translation at the University of Iowa, where I spent a delightful five weeks as the Fall 2023 Translator in Residence. Most of all, my deepest gratitude to Irma Pineda, for her consistent and unfailing benevolence, bravery, and brilliance. (Sobre todo, mi más profundo agradecimiento a Irma Pineda, por su constante e inquebrantable benevolencia, valentía y brillantez.)

Credits

POEMS

Poet and translator both thank the editors and staff of the literary journals where some of these English translations originally appeared, sometimes in slightly different versions, with the Didxazá and Spanish originals, all © Irma Pineda and Wendy Call unless otherwise noted:

Chicago Review, Fall 2018: [Where is the precise place], [Are you still a man?], [Mother   save yourself while you can], [Silence shattered], [Fear nested in the children's eyes], and [When the world pulled on its nightclothes].

ADI Magazine, Fall 2020: [Who are we now?], [Peace was our sister], and [You came with strangers to trample the grass].

Poetry, February 2022: [No wound hurts], [You declared war on us], and [My voice will weigh on you]. We are grateful that these translations (with Irma Pineda's translations to Spanish from Didxazá) were awarded the Poetry Foundation's John Frederick Nims Prize, for the best translations published by the journal during 2022.

IMAGES

Images on pages 4, 18, 22, and 90 by Angeles Torrejón; pages 16, 41, and 78 by Marco Antonio Cruz; pages xii, 1, 33, 46, 58, 64, and 96 by Heriberto Rodriguez.

IRMA PINEDA is among the most prominent Indigenous-language poets of the Americas, as well as a leading activist on human rights issues. She is the author of ten bilingual Didxazá-Spanish books of poetry, three books of poetry in Spanish, and three trilingual books in Wendy Call's English translation. Her poems are widely anthologized and have been translated into Estonian, French, German, Italian, Portuguese, Russian, and Serbian. She writes a biweekly newsmagazine column for the national Mexican newspaper *La Jornada* and was the first woman to serve as president of Mexico's National Organization of Writers in Indigenous Languages (ELIAC). From 2020 through 2022 Pineda served as one of two representatives of Latin America's Indigenous peoples at the United Nations Permanent Forum on Indigenous Issues, and she is currently a legislator in the Oaxacan State Congress. A long-time professor at the National Teachers University in Ixtepec, Oaxaca, Pineda is also a member of Mexico's National Academy for Artists and Creators (SNCA). She lives in her hometown of Juchitán, Oaxaca.

WENDY CALL is the author, co-editor, or translator of nine books. She co-edited the craft anthology *Telling True Stories: A Nonfiction Writers' Guide* and co-edits *Best Literary Translations,* an annual published by Deep Vellum each spring. Her creative nonfiction book *No Word for Welcome: The Mexican Village Faces the Global Economy* and her co-translation of Mikeas Sánchez's trilingual book *How to Be a Good Savage and Other Poems* both won Gold Medals from the International Latino Book Awards. Together with Irma Pineda, she received the 2022 John Frederick Nims Prize in Translation from the Poetry Foundation. A recent Translator in Residence at the University of Iowa and Fulbright Core (Faculty) Scholar to Colombia, she teaches nonfiction in the Rainier Writing Workshop MFA. She lives on Duwamish land, in Seattle, and on Zapotec and Mixtec land, in Oaxaca.

Praise for *Stolen Flower*

"A shocking book about a terrifying event, seen through the sharp and observant eyes of Mexican poet and activist Irma Pineda."
—María Baranda, author of *The New World Written*

"Irma Pineda's incantatory collection speaks truth to power in a voice that is prophetic, haunting, and hallucinatory, yet always brimming with humane compassion. Call's translations are translucent and cutting as glass, offering these poems that already live in twinned bodies of Didxazá and Spanish the clear-eyed vision of a third."
—Michael Bazzett, translator of *If Today Were Tomorrow,* selected poems of Humberto Ak'abal

"Irma Pineda's poetry is urgent, at once fierce and full of compassion. It brings us face to face with our times, denouncing the violence that so often tears our communities apart, and envisioning alternative futures as only poetry can."
—Cristina Rivera Garza, Pulitzer Prize–winning author of *Liliana's Invincible Summer: A Sister's Search for Justice*

"Childhood, her original memory, and her words are powerful ingredients in Irma, the poet, the woman, the human being, who reminds us how important it is not to forget our roots to survive."
—Juan Carlos Rulfo, documentary filmmaker

"Pineda's voice, ancestral echoes intertwined, stands forward with a timely poetic proposal on atrocities against Indigenous people. She builds sensitive tension in Zapotec, her tongue. Earthy, painful yet luminous. Never shy."
—Julia Santibáñez, winner of the Mario Benedetti International Poetry Award

"*Stolen Flower* is a harrowing call against brutality, already a classic among poems of witness. Pineda provides shelter for the uprooted and trampled flowers of Mexico's Indigenous nations."
—Anthony Seidman, translator of *Contra Natura* by Rodolfo Hinostroza

"Memory is metamorphosed into hope in Irma Pineda's mesmerizing poems. The lesson is clear: poetry might not save us from horror, but it offers us gravitas and even faith."
—Ilan Stavans, author of *Lamentations of Nezahualcóyotl: Nahuatl Poems*